I0134246

59 DAYS

TO HABIT CHANGE

By Jessica Wallaker

BLUE TRAIN
PUBLICATIONS

Published by Blue Train Publications in 2018

First Edition; First Printing

© 2018 Jessica Wallaker

rcksldgym.com

Cover background image from Engin_Akyurt

Inside images from Alexas_Fotos and StockSnap

All rights reserved. No part of this book may be reproduced or transmitted in any form or
by any means, including but not limited to information storage and retrieval systems,
electronic, mechanical, photocopy, recording, etc. without written permission from the
copyright holder.

ISBN **978-0-9996436-2-4**

HOW IT WORKS

- First, you'll write down your goals. What would you like to see happen in the next 59 days? Make it reasonable, yet enough of a challenge as well. What would you love to see come to light, or form into new habits?

- Next, explain exactly why you have these goals. Go into as much detail or just have key points if you want. Remember, you are doing this for you.

- After that, you start! Read each day, answer the prompts and see what happens. What will you find out if your goals are consciously being looked at and remembered for 59 days?

- Put down your stressors for the day, write down goals you want to see happen, and then whatever else your brain is saying. Sometimes we just need it out of our head in order to move forward. So what will you find out?

WHAT I FOUND

And here's the fun part, I wrote this as I committed 59 days to consciously thinking of the goals I wanted. And why 59? Check out #59cutoffdays and see what comes up. But these are my thoughts and realizations as I went through the days.

So it's not a bunch of random words that I put into a journal. These are the emotions, feelings, fears and excitements that I had throughout that time.

And in that time, I doubled my clientele, grew my business in ways I hadn't thought of, got back to good habits and started up new ones, opened my life to new possibilities and found a new love for myself I hadn't known before.

Those 59 days for me were so powerful and amazing, I wanted to share it with you!

So be open, don't stress, and see what happens if your goals are looked at for 59 days.

Again, what will you find out?

GOALS

- _____
  _____

- _____
  _____

- _____
  _____

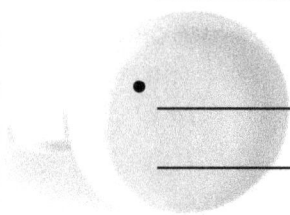

- _____
  _____

- _____
  _____

WHY

_____

_____

_____

_____

_____

_____

_____

_____

_____

_____

_____

_____

_____

_____

_____

_____

_____

_____

DAY 1

Every great dream begins with a dreamer. Always remember, you have within you the strength, the patience, and the passion to reach for the stars to change the world.

~Harriet Tubman

The first day is always doable. You're excited for change and to make this work. But knowing ahead of time that it won't always be easy is good to keep in mind. Do what you can. Look to try more than you have before, not complete perfection right away.

An accomplished day can look as small as doing one new thing and it not being a chore. Being open to whatever change looks like for you can make this process much easier.

TODAY'S THOUGHTS ___/___/___

STRESSORS: _____
_____
_____

GOALS: _____
_____
_____

BRAIN TALK: _____
_____
_____
_____
_____
_____
_____
_____
_____

DAY 2

You may realize that you're already starting to look at new ways to add in the habits you want to have. And that's great!

But be open and willing to start small. If it feels good to try another one, then do it.

But if you're happy with how yesterday went, try and do it again today. It can be exciting at first to do it all, right here right now.

If you really want these changes to last though, take it step by step.

You never know until you try.

TODAY'S THOUGHTS __/__/__

STRESSORS:_____

_____

_____

GOALS:_____

_____

_____

BRAIN TALK:_____

_____

_____

_____

_____

_____

_____

_____

_____

DAY 3

I've definitely learned that if you really want
something, just go for it, no matter how much
it scares you.

~Bethany Mota

Throughout this time together, you and your
journal, don't focus on perfection.

Think: What in my life is perfect all the time;
no problems or interferences ever?

If you work through this as if you need to
perfect it, you will hit more struggles and
roadblocks than if you went for mastery. If
you master a habit change, you know how to
work with it and make it fit in your day.

So be open and see how you can fit these new
habits in.

TODAY'S THOUGHTS ___/___/___

STRESSORS:_____
_____
_____

GOALS:_____
_____
_____

BRAIN TALK:_____
_____
_____
_____
_____
_____
_____
_____
_____

DAY 4

Some of your goals require small works in order to achieve them. Making small precise chisels in order to reveal your goal.

Sometimes that can be hard.

So start from the top, the finished project and work your way back; as small as you can go. Once you're there, that's where you start.

Small steps lead to large destinations.

Don't try to make it all happen at once.

TODAY'S THOUGHTS   __/__/__

STRESSORS:_____
_____
_____

GOALS:_____
_____
_____

BRAIN TALK:_____
_____
_____
_____
_____
_____
_____
_____
_____

DAY 5

When starting out on a new journey, aim for consistency, not perfection. A few days in, you may start to realize just what needs to change in your life in order to achieve your goals.

Is there something in the way of you moving forward?

Do you need to clean up in order to bring new things in?

Change can be hard, but it will be even harder if you try to bring in new habits without getting rid of old ones.

Is there anything you need to clear out in order to make room for the new?

TODAY'S THOUGHTS ___/___/___

STRESSORS:_____
_____
_____

GOALS:_____
_____
_____

BRAIN TALK:_____
_____
_____
_____
_____
_____
_____
_____
_____

DAY 6

What if you looked for one thing you are proud of today?

Sometimes we only see things that went wrong or weren't planned. Getting caught up in the negative can be hard to stay motivated.

So by finding even one thing that went right, it will help you stay positive.

The first few days can be super motivating, or up and down.

So, find something throughout the day that went well.

TODAY'S THOUGHTS ___/___/___

STRESSORS:_____
_____
_____

GOALS:_____
_____
_____

BRAIN TALK:_____
_____
_____
_____
_____
_____
_____
_____

DAY 7

There will be days when life tries to sneak in. Things are out of your control, you feel helpless, you want to do more, but feel you can't.

Do one good thing for you and enjoy it.

There will be days when you can only do the best with what you have. If that's today, pick your best option and congratulate yourself for it.

This is a journey down a path you've never gone before. Take it day by day, step by step.

Enjoy it.

TODAY'S THOUGHTS ___/___/___

STRESSORS:_____
_____
_____

GOALS:_____
_____
_____

BRAIN TALK:_____
_____
_____
_____
_____
_____
_____
_____
_____
_____

DAY 8

What will today bring?

Are you optimistic about the possibilities, or are you already stressing about them?

Go into today with an open mind. As much as we want to be in control of things and have them go our way, we really have little say in our day. You can either take this as defeat or a challenge.

If the latter, how can you make your circumstances work for you?

By deciding to take control of your reactions rather than your day, you ultimately come out with the upper hand.

So take control and don't stress.

TODAY'S THOUGHTS ___/___/___

STRESSORS:_____

_____

_____

GOALS:_____

_____

_____

BRAIN TALK:_____

_____

_____

_____

_____

_____

_____

_____

_____

DAY 9

What is most important to you?

Why is it that you want to make these changes?

Often when we start out on a new journey, we have great plans and high expectations. All good things!

But it's important to not stray away from the real reasons you're doing this. It's easy to get going and caught up in the goals, then forget the reason behind them.

So take a moment today to remember and reconnect with what it is you are really doing this for.

TODAY'S THOUGHTS   __/__/__

STRESSORS:_____
_____
_____

GOALS:_____
_____
_____

BRAIN TALK:_____
_____
_____
_____
_____
_____
_____
_____

DAY 10

What can you do today that you didn't yesterday? At least one thing.

Maybe an extra health food, that exercise you've been meaning to try, an email you haven't sent yet, the person you need to call back, or an appointment to set up.

Just one thing.

And if that's all you do today, it's one thing that hasn't happened yet.

This is a journey, not a race.

Pace, grow, do, try, enjoy.

TODAY'S THOUGHTS ___/___/___

STRESSORS:_____
_____
_____

GOALS:_____
_____
_____

BRAIN TALK:_____
_____
_____
_____
_____
_____
_____
_____
_____

DAY 11

What are you doing this for?

Are you trying to get your goals done quickly to gain the reward and say you finally did it?

Or do you want the lasting change?

If you truly want the forever change and for these things to just become who you are, they won't happen overnight.

Anything worth having is worth the time, so don't stress and rush it. Enjoy the ups and downs; take the experience of it all as some life realizations.

The more open you are to the process, the more will come your way.

TODAY'S THOUGHTS ___/___/___

STRESSORS:_____

_____

_____

GOALS:_____

_____

_____

BRAIN TALK:_____

_____

_____

_____

_____

_____

_____

_____

_____

DAY 12

As you go on this journey and work towards your goals, you already wrote down how it might affect you; your why.

But how might these new changes affect those around you? The people we cherish and have in our lives will be affected by any changes we make. We want it to be a positive change and usually it will be.

But what if it changes a relationship negatively or puts distance on that person? Are your goals important enough for you to be ok with that?

Making sure you are ok in all outcomes, opens up the chances and possibilities for change to happen.

So, is it worth it?

TODAY'S THOUGHTS __/__/__

STRESSORS:_____

_____

_____

GOALS:_____

_____

_____

BRAIN TALK:_____

_____

_____

_____

_____

_____

_____

_____

_____

DAY 13

Since we cannot change reality, let us change the eyes which see reality.

~ Nikos Kazantzakis

Some days you may not even touch your goals in the way you would like. But how can you make the most of it?

Life is never going to be perfect or just how you would like it.

But your openness and resiliency, to changes and things out of your control, will make these changes even easier to work with.

TODAY'S THOUGHTS

___/___/___

STRESSORS: _____

_____

_____

GOALS: _____

_____

_____

BRAIN TALK: _____

_____

_____

_____

_____

_____

_____

_____

_____

DAY 14

Life is 10% what happens to you and 90% how you react to it.
~Charles R. Swindoll

There will be days and moments, if there haven't already, where you will do the opposite of what it is you wanted to do. Where the goals and plans you have don't happen perfectly and you start to stray a bit.

But guess what? That's fine! You didn't fail, you aren't a bad person and you're actually growing.

It's deciding to make that choice to keep moving forward on this journey and realizing if your goals are still what you want to have in life.

So, is it still worth the risk?

TODAY'S THOUGHTS ___/___/___

STRESSORS:_____

_____

_____

GOALS:_____

_____

_____

BRAIN TALK:_____

_____

_____

_____

_____

_____

_____

_____

_____

DAY 15

Sometimes we feel that the things on our "To Do" list are more important to get done, than actual things we want to do. That once we get the important things accomplished, we'll have more time and availability to work on ourselves.

But is that list ever free? Once one thing is done, more will pile up and keep adding on.

There is no time like the present because tomorrow will never come. It turns into today, with it's own problems to bring.

So work on you amidst the chaos. You'll find it's not as hard as you think, and might actually help with the day to day we all tend to have.

TODAY'S THOUGHTS   __/__/__

STRESSORS:_____

_____

_____

GOALS:_____

_____

_____

BRAIN TALK:_____

_____

_____

_____

_____

_____

_____

_____

_____

DAY 16

What do you think will happen when you open yourself to change?

Will the things you wrote down come true?

What if I were to tell you more than you can imagine will come?

By being open, positive and continuously striving for success, you let anything else good come your way.

You may not realize until you slow down and take a step back, what all else there is that's happening.

Things that may go along with your goals, or are just there because you are.

TODAY'S THOUGHTS   __/__/__

STRESSORS:_____
_____
_____

GOALS:_____
_____
_____

BRAIN TALK:_____
_____
_____
_____
_____
_____
_____
_____
_____
_____

DAY 17

You set paths for yourself, but as you get older, things change.

~Ian McShane

This may seem like a silly thing to say, but it's true. Every step you take and each road you go, is going to look different than when you started.

The true challenge though is that we try to compare and cope with the change by comparing it to where we've been. You can't do that! You've never been in this same time, mind-set, situation and circumstances before.

To be able to grow and change, you have to be open to every new situation and place you are at.

TODAY'S THOUGHTS ___/___/___

STRESSORS:_____

_____

_____

GOALS:_____

_____

_____

BRAIN TALK:_____

_____

_____

_____

_____

_____

_____

_____

DAY 18

Some days you'll feel on top of it and ready to make strides; feeling inspired to take that next step.

Then there will be other days where you are dragging, uninspired and asking yourself why.

Don't sweat it!

We all have highs and lows. It's up to you how much you want to make of it.

By taking careful steps not to go too crazy on the highs, and doing what you must to keep at it on the lows.

This whole thing is for you. Don't forget that and cut yourself short.

You are worth so much more!

TODAY'S THOUGHTS ___/___/___

STRESSORS: _____
_____
_____

GOALS: _____
_____
_____

BRAIN TALK: _____
_____
_____
_____
_____
_____
_____
_____
_____

DAY 19

Life is what happens while we're busy making other plans.

~John Lennon

Don't get so caught up in life, that you forget what's happening today. For today is the only day you have any real say in.

Yesterday is done and you'll never get it back, while tomorrow is not guaranteed and will come with it's own problems.

So enjoy your time now and whatever control you have in the moment.

For whatever it is you are able to do today, will only benefit the unpredictable future.

TODAY'S THOUGHTS __/__/__

STRESSORS:_____
_____
_____

GOALS:_____
_____
_____

BRAIN TALK:_____
_____
_____
_____
_____
_____
_____
_____
_____

DAY 20

Do not dwell in the past, do not dream of the future, concentrate the mind on the present moment.

~Buddha

We spend more time planning, preparing and worrying for what may never happen, than what we actually have a say in. The more you give to the unknown, the less you get from the known.

By taking control and making things happen that you can, you are putting yourself in charge of what is in your hands.

You do have the power.

Now go and run with it.

TODAY'S THOUGHTS ___/___/___

STRESSORS:_____

_____

_____

GOALS:_____

_____

_____

BRAIN TALK:_____

_____

_____

_____

_____

_____

_____

_____

DAY 21

Take today to evaluate and look at your goals again. They've been sitting with you for a few weeks now.

Do they still represent where you want to go, what you want to do, who you want to be? If you need to change them, then do it!

As life progresses and we really look and see what we want, sometimes our goals need to change.

Either more specific, taking a new route, or letting one go in order to make room for another.

All are fine and progressive, because they show growth and leaning. Just keep tweaking.

TODAY'S THOUGHTS ___/___/___

STRESSORS:_____
_____
_____

GOALS:_____
_____
_____

BRAIN TALK:_____
_____
_____
_____
_____
_____
_____
_____
_____

DAY 22

What does your best future you look like?

What do they see, do, feel differently than you do now?

What would your future self tell you, here now?

Is it worth it, are they happy?

It can be hard and weird to picture your future self. But by doing this and really digging deep, you'll find out if it's worth all the hustle and work to reach those goals.

You'll find motivation and drive when you might not have before.

So check yourself and say hey to the future you.

TODAY'S THOUGHTS ___/___/___

STRESSORS:_____
_____
_____

GOALS:_____
_____
_____

BRAIN TALK:_____
_____
_____
_____
_____
_____
_____
_____
_____
_____

DAY 23

What is one goal, that if you changed and reached it, would mean the world to you?

Focus on that today.

Far too often we let life take control and distract us from the things we enjoy and crave.

So give yourself permission today to explore. Whether it's taking that class, calling that person, visiting that shop or just researching it more.

When you start to really chip away and add it into your life, you'll realize one of two things: either this is going to take more work than you might like, or you are fully willing to make it happen.

TODAY'S THOUGHTS ___/___/___

STRESSORS:_____
_____
_____

GOALS:_____
_____
_____

BRAIN TALK:_____
_____
_____
_____
_____
_____
_____
_____
_____

DAY 24

Are you happy with how things are going?

Odds are you've had at least one crummy day. And instead of taking it as defeat and walking away, take control.

What's one lesson, at least, that you can take away from a crummy day?

Maybe you're learning more of how you work and how you need to structure your day. Maybe you learn how much you can handle well and be productive.

Either way, it's one thing to notice lessons, but it's a whole other one to accept it.

So what will you take with you?

TODAY'S THOUGHTS ___/___/___

STRESSORS:_____
_____
_____

GOALS:_____
_____
_____

BRAIN TALK:_____
_____
_____
_____
_____
_____
_____
_____
_____

DAY 25

Don't forget why you're doing this.

Be selfish, this is YOUR time. These days are just keeping track and reminding you to be open. Things will come and go, opportunities and thoughts will change, but it's really all in your hands.

You can do this and you are. If you are still going through, being aware and mindful of this time you've given to yourself, change will happen.

Big or small, you're connecting and learning more about yourself than you ever would have before.

TODAY'S THOUGHTS ___/___/___

STRESSORS:_____
_____
_____

GOALS:_____
_____
_____

BRAIN TALK:_____
_____
_____
_____
_____
_____
_____
_____
_____
_____

DAY 26

Happiness is not something you postpone for the future; it is something you design for the present.

~Jim Rohn

Maybe you've had a few days of unexpected. You were shooting high for things to go a certain way, and they go the opposite.

Don't take it as defeat, take it as a lesson.

We learn best from the negatives in life because we are then more easily able to focus and refine our skills.

The only way you truly fail is by not learning from your mistakes.

TODAY'S THOUGHTS   __/__/__

STRESSORS:_____
_____
_____

GOALS:_____
_____
_____

BRAIN TALK:_____
_____
_____
_____
_____
_____
_____
_____
_____

DAY 27

Today is a new day, literally. You have, and never will experience or have one like this. Even if it's the same routine, same people, same places, it's different.

So everything you think and plan on happening, may not. Or it will be in a way that you weren't prepared for.

Even the slightest thing could be different, and it's still new to you.

So be open.

Embrace the unexpected things life offers and enjoy the adventure. Routines are nice, but the unexpected will challenge you to grow in ways you never imagined.

TODAY'S THOUGHTS __/__/__

STRESSORS:_____
_____
_____

GOALS:_____
_____
_____

BRAIN TALK:_____
_____
_____
_____
_____
_____
_____
_____
_____

DAY 28

What needs to change in order to have change happen?

Is it your schedule, time, place, people, set up, environment?

Are you willing to change things in order to get a new outcome?

Be honest with yourself.

Sometimes we aren't willing to change things to get what we want. Either your thinking and feelings will change so you can finally take those steps to have a successful goal. Or you will have to change your goal to fit your current situation.

Either way, you are growing and challenging yourself. Again., the only failure you can have is by not learning from life and your choices along the way.

TODAY'S THOUGHTS

___/___/___

STRESSORS:_____
_____
_____

GOALS:_____
_____
_____

BRAIN TALK:_____
_____
_____
_____
_____
_____
_____
_____
_____
_____

DAY 29

What are your gifts?
Be thoughtful with coming up with your answers.

What fills you with joy and energy?
What makes you excited and feels like you are living your true purpose; that anything is possible and dreams can become a reality?
You should be using your gifts, in some way, every day.

Now, how are your goals going to enhance your gifts? Have you thought about it?

If you're struggling with certain ones, it might be because they aren't the easy and natural thing for you to do, so enhancing them becomes difficult.

See how you can make your goals enjoyable and fulfilling for you, even in the smallest way.

TODAY'S THOUGHTS __/__/__

STRESSORS:_____
_____
_____

GOALS:_____
_____
_____

BRAIN TALK:_____
_____
_____
_____
_____
_____
_____
_____
_____

DAY 30

Try not to get lost in comparing yourself to others. Discover your gifts and let them shine!
~Jennie Finch

We are all destined for greatness, in our own way and our own journey. It won't look like everyone else, and that's fine. We are each made differently, with different goals, aspirations, loves, interests and fears.

By comparing yourself and judging your success against someone else's abilities is counter productive.

Focus on you, be selfish and show your true genius in all that you can do.

TODAY'S THOUGHTS ___/___/___

STRESSORS:_____
_____
_____

GOALS:_____
_____
_____

BRAIN TALK:_____
_____
_____
_____
_____
_____
_____
_____

DAY 31

Never lose yourself by becoming a victim of your circumstances. You have more say and more control than you realize.

It can be easy to get stuck in situations and feel like these are the cards you're dealt. You can decide to do something about it and change your outlook. And when you realize it's all up to you, things start to look brighter.

Options and opportunities appear when they never would have been an option before.

So what's holding you back? What's caging you from success?

Realize you hold the key to escape, and run for your life.

TODAY'S THOUGHTS ___/___/___

STRESSORS:_____
_____
_____

GOALS:_____
_____
_____

BRAIN TALK:_____
_____
_____
_____
_____
_____
_____
_____
_____
_____

DAY 32

Invest in you, because you're worth it.

Don't let other things get in the way of your success. In order to grow and thrive, we must be willing to make changes and take risks.

We don't let our money sit in the bank and expect it to grow. We invest and put it out there to multiply and benefit us.

So just like finances, we must invest in ourselves in order to see growth.

What do you see being beneficial and a big step for you? Are you willing to take the leap in order to have the benefit?

Yeah?

Then jump!

TODAY'S THOUGHTS ___/___/___

STRESSORS:_____

_____

_____

GOALS:_____

_____

_____

BRAIN TALK:_____

_____

_____

_____

_____

_____

_____

_____

_____

DAY 33

What have you noticed since being open to change?

For a months time now you have worked to try new things, set out on new tracks and see what happens.

Is it as hard as you thought? Have you tasted new change and are ready for more?

Sometimes all it takes is one good thing to make all other changes doable. It shows you how it doesn't have to be hard or scary. Change can be beneficial and completely unique for you.

So, what have you noticed?

TODAY'S THOUGHTS ___/___/___

STRESSORS:_____

_____

_____

GOALS:_____

_____

_____

BRAIN TALK:_____

_____

_____

_____

_____

_____

_____

_____

DAY 34

Life is a journey that must be traveled no matter how bad the roads and accommodations.

~Oliver Goldsmith

Are you trying to resurface a past habit? Are you trying to make it work for the current you?

Be careful not to get caught up in past expectations. Past habits worked well for that time. But current and future ones might look different.

Be open to the fact that you may need to be creative in order to make things work.

As long as you want it to happen, you'll find a way.

TODAY'S THOUGHTS ___/___/___

STRESSORS:_____
_____
_____

GOALS:_____
_____
_____

BRAIN TALK:_____
_____
_____
_____
_____
_____
_____
_____
_____

DAY 35

Do you ever allow yourself a day?

A day to yourself, to do what you want without feeling bad?

Whether it's a day trip somewhere you've been wanting to go, or binge watching a series you've been meaning to see, it's YOUR time.

We don't always allow ourselves time to just be. We may think we do, but then life stressors creep in, the "to do" list, family, events and even the goals we are trying to add in might be a stressor.

So what would happen if you allowed yourself 24 hours?

TODAY'S THOUGHTS ___/___/___

STRESSORS: _____
_____
_____

GOALS: _____
_____
_____

BRAIN TALK: _____
_____
_____
_____
_____
_____
_____
_____
_____

DAY 36

Life isn't fair and it never will be. We're told time and time again, yet we often forget.

When things go wrong, we feel sorry for ourselves and others in the form of pity. But these feeling help no one, they are a waste of energy.

We all have our own strengths and areas to grow, so who says these times don't offer just that.

Instead, focus on compassion and personal power. These things are uplifting and much more helpful in challenging situations.

Remember, life isn't, and never will be fair. YOU have the power to control how you respond to it.

TODAY'S THOUGHTS __/__/__

STRESSORS: _____
_____
_____

GOALS: _____
_____
_____

BRAIN TALK: _____
_____
_____
_____
_____
_____
_____
_____
_____

DAY 37

You have more control and more power than you believe. There is greatness in you if you're willing to let it out.

What's stopping you?

It is much easier to be stuck in the world of "woe is me" and feel powerless. But you have all the power in the world, it's just up to you to take control of it.

And this can be the hardest part; that you ultimately ARE in control of your life and how things turn out.

It just depends on how far you're willing to take it.

So, what's stopping you?

TODAY'S THOUGHTS ___/___/___

STRESSORS:_____
_____
_____

GOALS:_____
_____
_____

BRAIN TALK:_____
_____
_____
_____
_____
_____
_____
_____
_____
_____

DAY 38

Now and then it's good to pause in our pursuit
of happiness and just be happy.
~Guillaume Apollinaire

Don't get so caught up in life, goals, future
things, that you forget to see what you're
living in right now. Even if the situation or
circumstances aren't ideal, you can find
happiness and peace in your day-to-day life.

Enjoy the little things: buy some flowers,
watch the stars, notice the colors around you.

Take yourself out, buy that movie, eat that
cupcake.

Life is too short to only chase the future and
forget about the beautiful world you're in now.

TODAY'S THOUGHTS _/_/_

STRESSORS:_____
_____
_____

GOALS:_____
_____
_____

BRAIN TALK:_____
_____
_____
_____
_____
_____
_____
_____
_____

DAY 39

Life begins at the end of your comfort zone.
~Neale Donald Walsch

In order for change to happen, new things to come and for you to grow, comfort must be left. You can't, and never will change by doing the same thing.

In order to get to a point in life you've never been, you must be open and try things you never have before.

Yes, it can be daunting and intimidating, but how much do you want to see the positive change?

By stretching and growing, you truly find out what you're made of.

TODAY'S THOUGHTS __/__/__

STRESSORS:_____
_____
_____

GOALS:_____
_____
_____

BRAIN TALK:_____
_____
_____
_____
_____
_____
_____
_____
_____

DAY 40

What are your dreams, your aspirations, the big things that keep you up at night? The things you're afraid to tell others because they may seem unachievable.

Let your mind soar and wander; see where it goes. Sometimes our worldly experiences and expectations stop our daydreaming.

They stop our greatness and ability to believe the impossible is possible.

What would happen though, if you took off the chains of reality and let your imagination run wild.

What would you love most to do in this world?

TODAY'S THOUGHTS ___/___/___

STRESSORS:_____

_____

_____

GOALS:_____

_____

_____

BRAIN TALK:_____

_____

_____

_____

_____

_____

_____

_____

_____

_____

DAY 41

One's destination is never a place but rather a new way of looking at things.
~Henry Miller

Yesterday we let daydreaming happen again. Now, combining reality with wishes, what seems possible; challenging but possible?

Why does that dream in particular stick out to you? Why is that one so important?

Think it through, write it out and play with the idea. Just because it's a dream doesn't mean it can't be reality.

Sometimes it just takes new thinking and permission for yourself to be daring and adventurous.

So, what if?

TODAY'S THOUGHTS ___/___/___

STRESSORS:_____
_____
_____

GOALS:_____
_____
_____

BRAIN TALK:_____
_____
_____
_____
_____
_____
_____
_____

DAY 42

Never compare your journey with someone else's.

It's not a competition.

It is FAR too easy to think we aren't doing enough or we could be doing more. We see what others are doing, how far they are and think we are failing in comparison.

You have to be selfish and focus on you in this instance. Because when comparison and self-doubt come in, it is much easier to fall into defeat.

Unfollow, avoid, don't look or just ignore. Whatever it takes to get you in that positive space and moving forward towards YOUR goals.

It's your life, so make it the best you possibly can.

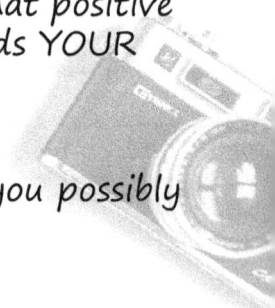

TODAY'S THOUGHTS ___/___/___

STRESSORS: _____

_____

_____

GOALS: _____

_____

_____

BRAIN TALK: _____

_____

_____

_____

_____

_____

_____

_____

_____

DAY 43

Success is no accident. It is hard work, perseverance, learning, studying, sacrifice and most of all, love of what you are doing or learning to do.

~Pele

Never stop learning, growing, exploring and being open to what is out there. The more you see and find, the more your journey will benefit from it.

We don't have all the answers, so it's best to go and find them. By doing this, you are also opening up yourself to share your wisdom with others.

No one is perfect and we'll never get to that point. But as long as you keep asking questions and looking for answers, your understanding of the world will be richly filled.

TODAY'S THOUGHTS ___/___/___

STRESSORS: _____
_____
_____

GOALS: _____
_____
_____

BRAIN TALK: _____
_____
_____
_____
_____
_____
_____
_____
_____

DAY 44

Look back at your goals you wrote down for these 59 days.

In a non-judgmental way, how are you doing on them?

Progress can look exactly how we expected, little steps forward, or in a much different way than expected.

All 3 are great though!

Because you are still trying and picking away at these habits, and that's exactly what habits look like.

They are a part of your life that is important, but flexible. You start becoming an expert at making it work and fit in your life.

So don't get frustrated if it doesn't go exactly as planned. It just proves you are still trying to make it work for you.

TODAY'S THOUGHTS ___/___/___

STRESSORS:_____
_____
_____

GOALS:_____
_____
_____

BRAIN TALK:_____
_____
_____
_____
_____
_____
_____
_____
_____

DAY 45

What do you need to do for yourself today?

Too often we go-go-go without realizing we are taking too much from ourselves. That's encouraged in our society, to push yourself, improve and be better.

All great things, but if you aren't doing something just for you and fulfilling your needs and wants on a deeper level, then you truly aren't giving your best self to others.

In order to do that, we must take some time back for ourselves and fulfill our needs.

Sometimes 5 minutes is all it takes if there's no time. You give so much to others, you can afford at least 5 minutes to you.

TODAY'S THOUGHTS ___/___/___

STRESSORS:_____

_____

_____

GOALS:_____

_____

_____

BRAIN TALK:_____

_____

_____

_____

_____

_____

_____

_____

DAY 46

Do you treat life like an emergency? That if things don't get done just how you think they should, it's failure?

Think about it, what's the worse thing that could happen?

Have you heard the saying, even when you die, your inbox will still be full?

I won't deny that there are things in life that are stressful. It's when you turn any little thing that isn't perfect into stress that there's a problem.

Don't forget that you're only human. Heck, not even technology is perfect.

So don't hold yourself to such high standards that you can't appreciate your own faults.

Embrace the messes and do the best you can.

TODAY'S THOUGHTS ___/___/___

STRESSORS:_____
_____
_____

GOALS:_____
_____
_____

BRAIN TALK:_____
_____
_____
_____
_____
_____
_____
_____
_____

DAY 47

What makes you excited about your goals?

This question should be fun, full of adventure and opportunity. Thinking of your goals happening and coming true should give you that drive and excitement you had when you first wrote them down.

If you're having trouble answering this question though, why did you write down these goals in the first place? It should be easy and exciting to think about the future.

Dreams are coming true, potential is being lived and possibilities are endless.

This doesn't mean the journey will be easy, far from it actually. But, it will make the trek much more worth it.

TODAY'S THOUGHTS ___/___/___

STRESSORS:_____
_____
_____

GOALS:_____
_____
_____

BRAIN TALK:_____
_____
_____
_____
_____
_____
_____
_____
_____

DAY 48

There will be days when your goals aren't able to be met in the way you would like them to be. It could be due to work, events, travel, family or just the unexpected times life throws your way.

That doesn't mean they get a free pass and you just move on.

Be creative, see how you can incorporate those things in when times aren't ideal.

If you do this, goals and habits will stick much better when you're able to be flexible and creative.

New habits won't seem as intimidating to keep.

Life isn't perfect, so your goals won't always be either.

TODAY'S THOUGHTS   __/__/__

STRESSORS:_____

_____

_____

GOALS:_____

_____

_____

BRAIN TALK:_____

_____

_____

_____

_____

_____

_____

_____

_____

DAY 49

I can't change the direction of the wind, but I can adjust my sails to always reach my destination.

~Jimmy Dean

By taking control of your actions, responses and thinking, you are taking control of your life. We hear this over and over again, but rarely take it to heart.

It's hard to hear and accept that you truly are in control. We want so badly to be in charge and have a perfect life, but when we're told to actually take charge to make it happen, we find excuses.

It can be hard to take on that responsibility of everything happening in life, but knowing you have a say does make things a little easier.

So embrace your journey, accept your strength and just keep trying.

TODAY'S THOUGHTS ___/___/___

STRESSORS: _____
_____
_____

GOALS: _____
_____
_____

BRAIN TALK: _____
_____
_____
_____
_____
_____
_____
_____
_____

DAY 50

There's a saying that if everyone stood in a circle and put their problems in the middle to exchange, everyone would take their own problems back.

You've been given your difficulties and triumphs, positives and negatives because you can handle them. It may not seem like it all the time, but there is a bigger plan and purpose for it all.

The journey you're on and the goals you have will come with struggles, but the outcome is more than worth it.

Learn and grow more than you imagined, you just have to get past the growing pains.

TODAY'S THOUGHTS ___/___/___

STRESSORS:_____
_____
_____

GOALS:_____
_____
_____

BRAIN TALK:_____
_____
_____
_____
_____
_____
_____
_____
_____

DAY 51

Don't let the negativities of life take your sparkle. Don't let your doubts dim your shine.

You've been given this life, your struggles and your passions for a reason. It would be a shame and a loss to the world to not show them.

Everything will fight against you to keep them down; to stop them from helping the world.

It is up to you to let them though.

By allowing your potential to be free, you are giving your truest self permission to be seen.

Embrace the fear, for the world could use a little extra light.

TODAY'S THOUGHTS ___/___/___

STRESSORS:_____
_____
_____

GOALS:_____
_____
_____

BRAIN TALK:_____
_____
_____
_____
_____
_____
_____
_____
_____

DAY 52

Past failures do not depict future outcomes.
Just because it happened before, doesn't mean
it will always be that way.

You are changing your outlook, your thinking,
big and small. Those changes are the things
that will depict your future.

If you truly want success and a positive
outcome, these small steps towards your goals
are exactly what will get you there.

It is never too late to start or to try again.
And it is never a failure if you don't quit; it is
just one more bump on your walk through life.

TODAY'S THOUGHTS ___/___/___

STRESSORS:_____
_____
_____

GOALS:_____
_____
_____

BRAIN TALK:_____
_____
_____
_____
_____
_____
_____
_____

DAY 53

Never underestimate the small steps.

There will be days when it seems like an uphill battle with no end in sight.

But the more you keep working, trucking forward and making progress, you will see changes happening.

They may come all at once or they may be small steps where you start to realize the benefit now.

So look back.

How have your goals been changing and making an appearance in your life?

Is it exactly how you thought when starting out, or have you been changing along the way as well?

TODAY'S THOUGHTS ___/___/___

STRESSORS:_____

_____

_____

GOALS:_____

_____

_____

BRAIN TALK:_____

_____

_____

_____

_____

_____

_____

_____

_____

DAY 54

We are coming in on the last few days here. Have you been working on all of your goals?

Go back and look, and really look.

Are those things you wrote down still important to you or have your thoughts and feelings changed about them?

Take today to review.

You started this journey for a reason; you wrote down those things because they had importance.

Explore and see if you can find it again.

TODAY'S THOUGHTS ___/___/___

STRESSORS:_____
_____
_____

GOALS:_____
_____
_____

BRAIN TALK:_____
_____
_____
_____
_____
_____
_____
_____
_____

DAY 55

Plan, prep, prepare, think of worse-case-scenario, don't get hurt, etc.

Far too often by being beyond prepared for the future, we miss out on it.

We take too much time getting ready that we miss chances to take.

Have you missed any of those?

What would happen if you didn't skip out on possibilities?

Give it a try next time. You may be surprised how ready you were. And if not, well, life itself is the greatest teacher. So you're in good hands.

TODAY'S THOUGHTS __/__/__

STRESSORS:_____
_____
_____

GOALS:_____
_____
_____

BRAIN TALK:_____
_____
_____
_____
_____
_____
_____
_____
_____
_____

DAY 56

Don't be afraid to take that leap.

You may start to see things opening up and being more available to you. Or maybe it's been happening.

Don't be afraid to take the leap. It's scary, it's unfamiliar and it's so thrilling. You gain more confidence and control as you take the chance and see what happens.

By letting go, you are also giving yourself intense freedom and trust that you CAN and you WILL be successful in some way, shape or form.

So have fun with your new branch of freedom.

You can do it!

TODAY'S THOUGHTS ___/___/___

STRESSORS:_____

_____

_____

GOALS:_____

_____

_____

BRAIN TALK:_____

_____

_____

_____

_____

_____

_____

_____

_____

DAY 57

What are all the positive things going on?

Sometimes we can easily get caught up in what we need to do, what's going wrong, or even all that's going right.

Don't forget to enjoy the journey.

Even when everything is going great you can still stress and worry.

Practice taking a step back and look at all the good happening in your life. And if that seems like a hard place to start, don't forget you woke up today.

The world is a better place because you are taking up space.

TODAY'S THOUGHTS ___/___/___

STRESSORS:_____

_____

_____

GOALS:_____

_____

_____

BRAIN TALK:_____

_____

_____

_____

_____

_____

_____

_____

_____

DAY 58

What are you learning?

What are you experiencing?

Have you stuck with this?

Have you found out things about yourself?

As you go through life and take this experimental mentality with you, you might notice things changing.

You might notice you aren't as stressed as you've been before.

You realize you can accomplish things and make them work for you.

Even in the smallest sense, you are making things happen.

So keep striving forward and know you have the power in you to make things great.

TODAY'S THOUGHTS ___/___/___

STRESSORS:_____
_____
_____

GOALS:_____
_____
_____

BRAIN TALK:_____
_____
_____
_____
_____
_____
_____
_____
_____

DAY 59

Don't stop here.

But congrats on getting here!
Whether you accomplished all your goals, or just made strides at achieving them, you stuck with this. And that's huge in itself!

So don't stop here.

Use this momentum, use this proof to yourself that it is possible to make changes over time. That you can stick with something, no matter what that looks like.

You are, can and will do great things.

Just keep on picking away, making strides and again, don't stop here.

TODAY'S THOUGHTS ___/___/___

STRESSORS:_____

_____

_____

GOALS:_____

_____

_____

BRAIN TALK:_____

_____

_____

_____

_____

_____

_____

_____

_____

LOOK BACK

Go through and see your journey.
What happened?

_____

_____

_____

_____

_____

_____

_____

_____

_____

_____

_____

_____

_____

_____

_____

_____

LOOK BACK

Was it what you expected?

_____

_____

_____

_____

_____

_____

_____

_____

_____

_____

_____

_____

_____

_____

_____

_____

_____

_____

LOOK BACK

How do you feel at the end of this experiment now?

_____

_____

_____

_____

_____

_____

_____

_____

_____

_____

_____

_____

_____

_____

_____

LOOK BACK

Will you continue on with your goals to make them solid habits?

_____
_____
_____
_____
_____
_____
_____
_____
_____
_____
_____
_____
_____
_____
_____

LOOK BACK

What do you think you need to make sure you continue on with it?

_____

_____

_____

_____

_____

_____

_____

_____

_____

_____

_____

_____

_____

_____

_____

_____

_____

GOALS

- _____
  _____

- _____
  _____

- _____
  _____

- _____
  _____

- _____
  _____

WHY

_____
_____
_____
_____
_____
_____
_____
_____
_____
_____
_____
_____
_____
_____
_____
_____
_____
_____

ABOUT THE AUTHOR

Confident and Fit Coaching
confidentandfit.com

Jessica Wallaker is a young entrepreneur in the making. From starting her own coaching business, Confident and Fit Coaching, in her early 20's to writing her first journal in 2017. Her main goal with coaching and writing is to help people better understand what it is that they want to get out of their life. Showing them that health doesn't have to be one separate compartment in their hectic schedule; it can be fun, enjoyable and also stress free. Who would've thought!

If you are interested in any coaching or upcoming programs, please go to rcksldgym.com

ALSO BY JESSICA WALLAKER

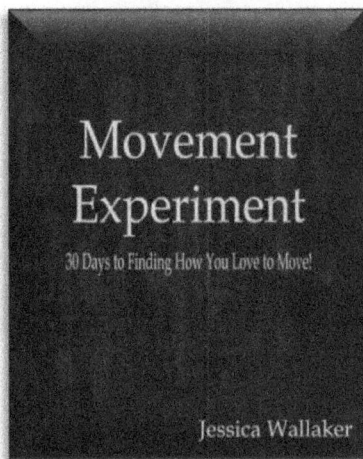

Food Experiment
30 Days to Finding What You Love to Eat!
Jessica Wallaker

Movement Experiment
30 Days to Finding How You Love to Move!
Jessica Wallaker

Available at amazon.com
Be sure to check us out at
confidentandfit.com for new additions
coming soon!

www.ingramcontent.com/pod-product-compliance
Lightning Source LLC
LaVergne TN
LVHW091223080426
835509LV00009B/1136